D1566445

GARIFUNA 4 CHILDREN

Coloring Book

Created by Isidra Sabio

Dedicated to the all Garifuna children around the world!

Garifuna-4-Children Coloring Book

AJANI PUBLISHING

516-495-6426
P.O BOX 30683
Elmont, NY 11003
Ajani.publishing@Gmail.com

www.trishsthill.com

ISBN: 978-0-9824852-5-5 (softcover)

Published by Ajani Publishing

Cover and Illustrations by Isidra Sabio

To order copies of this book

www.amazon.com

www.facebook.com/AfroLatinPublishing

Printed in USA

Introducción

The Garifuna language originated in the Island of St. Vincent prior to the Garifuna people's exile to Central America in 1797. The language is currently spoken by more than 100,000 Garifunas around the world, mainly, in Honduras, Guatemala, Belize, and in the United States.

On May 21st 2001, the UNESCO declared the Garifuna Language, Dance, and Music a "**Masterpiece of the Oral and Intangible Heritage of Humanity**".

This coloring book was designed for children to have fun while learning the Garifuna language.

Achubara

Saltar

To Jump

Óuchaha

Pescar

Fishing

Eiga

Comer

To Eat

Ágawa

Bañar

To Bathe

Ábuogua

Cocinar

To cook

Arumuga

Dormir   To sleep

Áfuliha

Bucear

To Dive

Éibagua

Correr

To Run

Bugudura

Tortuga

Tortoise

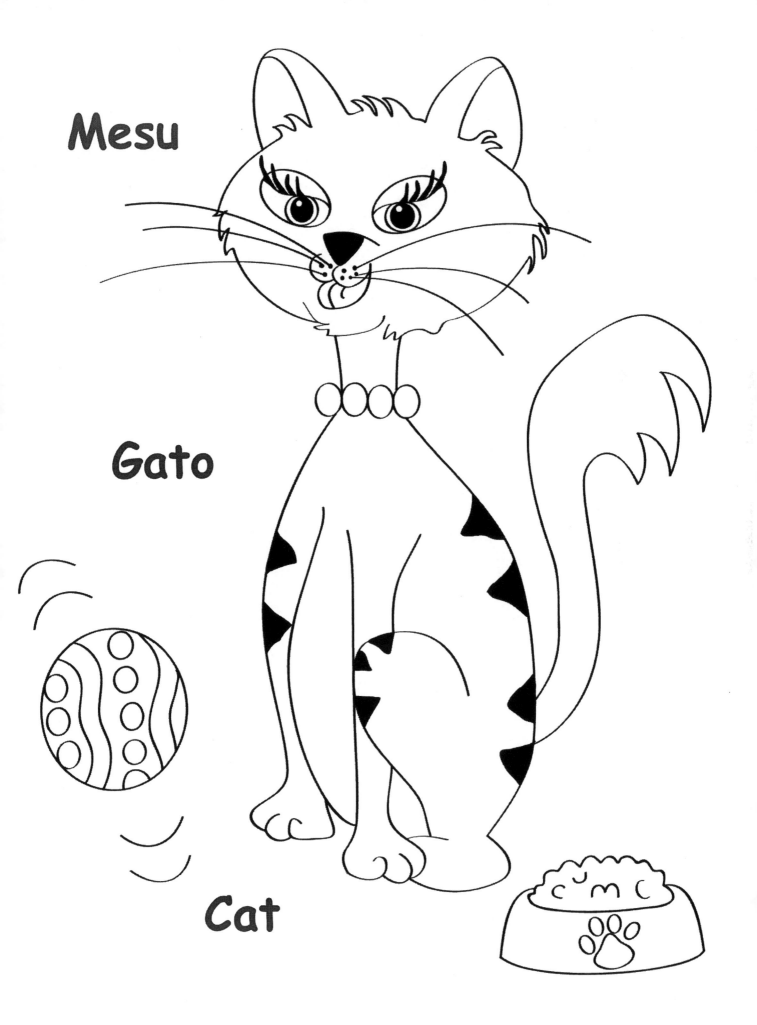

Gurewegi

Loro

Parrot

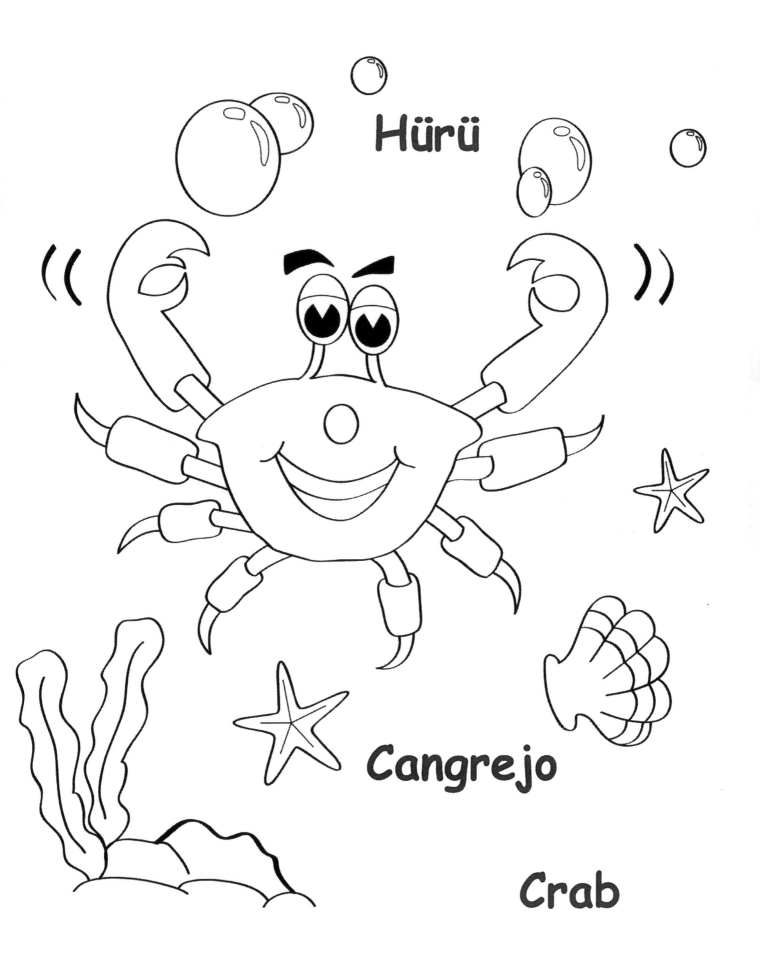

Hürü

Cangrejo

Crab

Üduraü

Peces

Fish

Éigini

Comida

Food

Hati

Luna

Moon

Weyu

Sol

Sun

Würi

Mujer

Woman

Eyeri

Hombre   Man

Isidra Sabio was born and raised in the Garifuna community of Cristales in Trujillo, Honduras. Isidra holds a Master of Science degree from Louisiana State University. In 2007, Isidra received a "Scientific Contribution" award presented by the President of Honduras. Currently, Isidra works as a Public Health researcher in the United States.

Isidra began drawing and illustrating when she was a little girl, she has several books in print for children and has created a line of greeting cards through her publishing company Afro-Latin Publishing, Inc.

41246995R00017

Made in the USA
Middletown, DE
07 March 2017